The Wandering Soul: Lost in the Words

By Dani Johnson

Maxine,
I hope that you enjoy this.
Thank you for your support.

Love,
Dani

Type of Work:	Text
Registration Number / Date:	TX0008726508 / 2019-03-30
Application Title:	The Wandering Soul: Lost in the Words.
Title:	The Wandering Soul: Lost in the Words.
Copyright Claimant:	Dani Johnson, United States. ©
Date of Creation:	2018
Date of Publication:	2018-11-17 ©
Nation of First Publication:	United States
Authorship on Application:	Dani Johnson; Domicile: United States; Citizenship: United States. Authorship: text.
Rights and Permissions:	Dani Johnson
Copyright Note:	Basis for Registration: Collective Work
ISBN:	9781731360199

Dedicated to my mom. Who has continuously
encouraged me to
follow my path,
however crooked or bumpy.
You have loved me always, never giving up.
What am I going to do with you?
Keep me, Keep me…

She found herself.
Not when she was
Following direction,
But when she was lost.

She wonders if he knows,
What it took for her to fall.
The heart she protected so dearly,
Was now a crumbling wall.

To know her,
Is to understand the beautiful chaos
That makes her who she is.
There's a fire inside her,
A passion for living.
If she loves you,
Know that it won't be easy.
For she is risking it all,
To open her heart completely.

What do you do?
With the eyes that tell a story.
She held it all together,
Like the sun in all of its glory.
She stood on top of that mountain,
Never looking back,
For the girl who dreamt the impossible,
Turns out, the impossible was her knack.

The thing about her you see,
Different from others,
She was a rare breed.
She believed in things that others couldn't dream,
So passionate about life,
Many called her their sunshine beam.
If she loves you,
Know this love is made of fire.
Word to the wise,
Never doubt her power.

Feed your dreams she said,
As they walked through the trees.
She always followed this advice,
Living for her heart,
Living to be free.
As they walked hand in hand,
The beauty of nature swallowing them whole.
For it is always in the woods,
Where one can soothe the soul.

Unapologetically passionate,
With all things in life.
They tried calming her spirit,
Forgetting her insatiable drive.
Traditional she was not,
In love and the like.
The reasons that they fell for her,
Were the same that they took flight.
She'd continue to give regardless,
Forgiving those in her past.
For she believed in kindness,
And a romance that would last.

Climb that mountain,
Enjoy that kiss.
Fingertips upon skin,
This is bliss.
Discover magic,
Tap into your senses.
Expand your mind,
There are no fences.

Understand me, she said,
I am made of things one couldn't fathom.
I'll take your words of rejection,
And run with them like a phantom.
Building strength from humility,
A talent she has perfected.
For it's the weakness seen in others,
That can be easily detected.
Run she will not,
From problems that arise.
She a warrior through and through,
You can see it in her eyes.

Embrace the wonder,
Embrace the touch.
Give into the unknown,
Give into that rush.
The high you feel is endless,
The high you can't resist.
This is the exchange of energies,
This is the meaning of bliss.

Silly little one,
You tried to hide your truths.
The person you really are,
You failed to introduce.
Not sure of who to be,
So you change from day to day.
Wake up and be yourself,
Say what you have to say.
Love the energies you vibe with,
Bring peace along with you.
Those who cross your path,
Will appreciate the sunshine to.

She wakes every morning,
A smile on her face.
Excited for the future,
A feeling she can taste.
She's unlike any you've known,
To some appearing strange.
Radiating the energy of peace,
The opposite of living in a cage.
Running wild with her dreams,
Adventure pulsing through her veins.
Living only to be free,
Letting the universe take the reins.

As she walk through the woods,
Her heart is at peace.
A place she can lose herself,
A place she is never weak.
Where the wild understands her,
And the trees always speak.
This place that she belongs,
Is forever willing to teach.
Listen as the wind tells stories of the past,
For it is in Mother Nature,
Where you will always find your path.

Hold her tight,
For she likes to wander.
Deep into the woods,
Where her mind begins to wonder.
Let's get lost, she said,
As she looked into his eyes.
Not all live for this thrill,
Not all are ready for this ride.
She'll take you on journeys,
Unlike you've ever seen.
Living for the moment,
Living out their dreams.

Mind meets mind,
A seduction beyond words.
Tease her with your thoughts,
And the dreams of other worlds.
Devour her curiosity,
And swallow her desires.
She will feed your soul,
With a passion made of fire.

These mountains are endless,
A beauty beyond words.
She took him by the hand,
Guiding him through the curves.
In his eyes,
Something she'd never seen.
A lust for life,
A man who dreams.
His movements tantalizing,
Provoking a hunger within her.
It's in this place of possibilities,
Where they didn't mind to linger.

Soul to soul,
Thought for thought.
This is the moment,
Your mind was caught.
Words sensually caress,
Places you've kept hidden.
Yearning to dive deeper,
Realizing you are smitten.
Behind the physical,
Beyond their touch,
This is where it begins,
This is the rush.

She craves,
She wishes.
She dares,
She's distant.
Pleasure her mind,
Desire her needs.
She wants to explore,
You leave her intrigued.

Save them, she said,
Before it's too late.
They belong to the wild,
Surviving is their fate.
Please don't buy that piece,
A life lost for no reason.
They don't hunt us down,
No matter what they season.
They were here before us,
Leaving beauty in their wake.
Please see the importance,
Their lives are not yours to take.

Over the bridge,
And past the wall.
There's a place that she goes,
A place she can fall.
Exposing her insides,
Screaming her truths.
She lives for this thrill,
The outside world seeming mute.
The trees always listen,
As she tells her tales.
At home in this place,
She loves without fail.

What is a kiss?
If it is not deep.
What is a risk?
If you don't leap.
What is passion?
If it's not consuming.
What is living?
If you're not pursuing.
What is a touch?
If not done with purpose.
What is love?
If it's not pass the surface.

She's a flame,
A fire that can't be put out.
She feeds your drive,
And removes your doubt.
Sacrificing her own,
To see you succeed.
She holds her head high,
And encourages your dreams.
Recognizing her strength,
Took years to understand.
She encompassed all the love in the world,
Held in a mother's hand.

Unlike any other,
A rare breed indeed.
She appreciated the night,
And devoured her dreams.
Believing in things,
Others couldn't see.
She gave all she had,
Like a bird she was free.
An old soul deep within,
Her smile everlasting.
There was kindness on her lips,
Her spell she was casting.

What is it that you see in her?
Perhaps a fire like your own.
Is it the way she laughs,
Enticing down to the bone.
Maybe it's the way she looks at you,
Like you are all who exists.
Maybe it's her mind,
Maybe it's her kiss.
Could it be the way she holds your stare?
A match of seductive gaze.
Or is it the way she gets your soul,
Keeping up through your winding maze.

She doesn't fall easily,
Protecting her most precious parts.
For you to get close enough,
Discover her from the start.
More than the curves,
Of the roads you'd like to take.
Her mind is the key,
To her soul you'll captivate.

Late night talks,
Sensual caresses.
Thoughts exchanged,
More than expected.
This place she could stay,
A need within her captured.
He handled her with care,
And devoured her with passion.
An anchor she'd be,
For days he couldn't bear.
In her arms he'd lay,
Dreams they would share.

You thought about her,
A soul like your own.
Trusting her intentions,
Taking you into the unknown.
She took the time to heal,
The wounds that ran so deep.
Will you do the same?
Her secrets yours to keep.
A love she will give you,
Unlike any you've ever known.
Protecting your guarded heart,
Giving it a place to call home.

Foolish one,
Pay close attention.
Your words are good,
If matched with affection.
Blind are the ones,
Who only see themselves.
You can't expect the sun,
If you shadow someone else.

Positive thoughts,
Radiating light.
Chances given,
Soon take flight.
Delicate thoughts,
Sent out with force.
Power of the mind,
Takes its course.
Lost you are not,
For it lies within you.
Strength you possess,
The will to continue.

Threw her heart in the ocean,
To see if it would float.
Silly little thing,
Came back with a note.
I am full of compassion,
I am full of strength.
But do not test my loyalty, it said.
For next time I will sink.

Wear and tear,
Grin and bear.
Lesson learned,
Pages turn.
Love exists,
It's in the kiss.
Days are longer,
Feeling stronger.
Positive thoughts,
Can't be bought.
Find your rhyme,
Give it time.
Watch for clues,
This is your muse.

Here's your dame,
She's all but tame.
Living loud,
Head in the clouds.
Rebel heart,
She digs her arts.
Insatiable ambitions,
Trusting her intuition.
Loyal to the core,
She's happily yours.

Praying they won't see,
The scars that run so deep.
The ugly lost inside,
The flaws you just can't hide.
It's a part of who you are,
Etched just below the surface.
Do you think they know?
You tried to find its purpose.
Wanting to find a new home,
For the nightmares that no longer fit.
Here in this place you designed,
The memories, they sit.

Beyond the words,
Action is what she hoped for.
Through fear,
Strength is what she became.
Countless times,
Her breath taken from her.
Only one more mountain to climb,
She told herself.
But the journeys my dear,
Are infinite.

She painted a picture,
For everyone to see.
The person she truly is,
Who she knew herself to be.
Then those that knew her,
Added their parts too.
The way they saw her,
As the picture grew.
She began to notice,
Parts she didn't recognize.
Seeing herself clearly,
Through someone else's eyes.
Take note of those dear to you,
For they will help you see.
The person you truly are,
The person you hope to be.

When I was 10,
My world began.
Learning from the trees,
All that I could be.
A strength I'd long to possess,
The sky, a need to caress.
A shelter in which they gave,
As a child, a home I made.
Knowing a life before this,
This place,
My heart had purpose.

Where would we be without the poets?
The ones who expose their truths.
Written are the words,
Crafted since their youth.
Passionate and raw,
Laying it all out to bear.
A diary if you will,
Hearts so selflessly shared.

Where does it all go?
Once you say it out loud.
Does it flutter into space?
Or land down on the ground.
Do the wounds heal themselves?
After the words are said.
Or do they rip apart some more,
Creating doubt inside your head.
Maybe after a while,
When time does its dance.
Memories become more distant,
You'll have a fighting chance.
It won't always feel like this,
The pain that sits on your chest,
For you were meant to conquer,
And survive all the rest.

She could only listen,
Her words seeming invalid.
She could only watch,
As history became the habit.

She's a wildflower,
In a store full of roses.
Taking the road less traveled,
Curiosity she's always chosen.
The thing about her,
An old soul indeed.
Hands in the earth,
Remaining wild is her need.
She speaks to the animals,
Of every shape and size.
A longing to protect,
A love spoken through our eyes.

He said, be a book,
So I can read you.
The parts she hides,
He wants to see too.
Never in her life,
Has she wanted such a thing.
To share her deepest thoughts,
Knowing what that could bring.
He brought out the best,
Understood her to a T.
The day she let go,
He began to read.

Keeping her lips sealed,
So the words don't escape.
She's a writer after all,
Spilled ink is her fate.
A collector of thoughts,
Marinating in her mind.
She observes from afar,
The Truth will speak in time.

A rebel,
Writing what you can't say.
Here she is safe,
To expose their evil ways.
A monster if you will,
The ugly seeping through.
Only for so long,
Before others see it too.
Patience it will take,
To sit back and watch.
This rebel is waiting,
Inside her web of words they'll be caught.

It's not always easy,
Waiting your turn.
They say patience is a virtue,
As the memories burn.
Doing what she does best,
Insides poured out on the page,
Trying to heal the wounds,
That others left in their rage.
They say time heals all,
Believing this to be true.
So she'll write for them,
Until they can feel it too.

A beginning and an end,
These opposites collide.
Ready for the new,
To the past,
We say goodbye.

Words unspoken,
Maybe one day.
You'll get a piece,
They hid away.
One day maybe,
They'll look at you.
You'll be the thing,
They're afraid to lose.

Inconvenient,
Out of the way.
Speak your mind,
While others play.
Cards of life,
Your hands been dealt.
This game takes patience,
As the ice melts.

A figment of the imagination,
That is what she became.
A life no longer hers,
That much passion can't be tamed.
Writing until it makes sense,
One word at a time.
Who she really is,
Revealed only through her eyes.

Adoration, admiration,
Like and love.
Romance and comedy,
Qualities within one.
Unable to go without,
This magnetic pull.
A feeling of certainty,
Hearts so completely full.

Eyes as bright as the stars,
Mesmerizing deep within.
Radiating heat,
The energy of the sun built in.
The planets have aligned,
The moon casting its glow.
These two are made by design,
Their signs written in stone.

Ancient minds are lurking,
Beside you every day.
You wouldn't know to look at them,
Mysterious is where they stay.
Carrying years of wisdom,
Of lives they've lived before.
It is in their curious eyes,
That keeps them opening every door.

What is it you're looking for?
Do you even know?
Is it written in the stars?
Or found down below.
Is it something you can taste?
Or feel it with a touch.
You can't deny the pull,
This thing you want so much.
Don't forget this feeling,
The one that fuels your drive.
Never let this go,
This thing that keeps you alive.

History repeats itself,
Or so they say.
She's seen the proof,
Day after day.
Drawing them in,
They feed off her light.
Indulging her passions,
Before they take flight.
A one in a million,
Forever she'll be.
Her wild eyes have the power,
Of setting them free.

Catching the eyelash,
She made her wish.
Blew it away,
That's when they kissed.
Perhaps it was magic,
Or maybe it was fate.
Knowing this was a chance,
She was meant to take.
Don't hold your breath,
Or wait for the fall.
Be alive in these moments,
You weren't born to crawl.

What did she see?
When she looked into his eyes.
Was he a man full of dreams?
Was there a part of him he hides?
How about the way,
He looks after a long day.
Has he any clue,
She respects his deepest views.
His drive she admires,
One matching her own.
Intrigued by his thoughts,
Welcoming the unknown.

What is it about her?
That drives you absolutely wild.
Is it the way she laughs from her soul,
Or maybe her contagious smile.
Perhaps it's her mind,
Does she make you want to think?
Once you've gotten a taste,
She's all you'll want to drink.
Hold on to a love like hers,
You'll never know another.
For her heart is unconditional,
Unlike any other.

She wanted him,
The man inside.
Not who he portrays,
The one he tries to hide.
She'd take his fears,
And fuel his drive.
He did the same for her,
But doesn't realize.
He'd met his match,
A heart like his own.
She only hoped the past,
Had not turned him to stone.

The thing about her,
She had to write until she was free.
Her raw emotions on the page,
For everyone to see.
That smile, oh that smile,
An undeniable strength.
For those she adored,
She went to great lengths.
Hurt she had been,
Far too many to count.
You wouldn't know to look at her,
The eyes never revealing doubt.
The moment you think you know her,
She surprises you with a turn.
It's the fire in her heart,
For her passions she would burn.

She did it again,
Playing the part.
Always understanding,
Had it down to an art.
Ready as ever,
She remained open minded.
Here's hoping this time,
She wouldn't be blindsided.

She listened as they spoke,
Words getting lost on the way.
She tried to swallow them down,
I want you, is all she could say.

If she were yours,
You know how it goes.
You'd do what others couldn't,
What others didn't know?
If she were yours,
You'd sweep her off her feet.
You'd give her what she craved,
From her body you'd feel the heat.
If she were yours,
She'd never have to wonder.
Maybe one day she would,
Maybe one day they wouldn't wander.

You know that ugly part inside,
With all those broken pieces.
The one you just can't recognize,
Not even in the creases.
You tried to dig them out,
The further they went in.
You wanted to go back there,
And erase what has been.
These moments swallow you whole,
Sticking to your bones.
You want to rip them out,
But you'd leave your soul,
Without a home.
They say it will get better,
That time heals the past.
You hope that they are right,
This ugly just can't last.

Hold her tight,
Breathe her in.
She needs this now,
From where she's been.
Get lost in her,
She'll show you where.
A dream like state,
Skin so bare.
Hold her tight,
Never let go.
You need her too,
You just didn't know.

It was cold last night,
Without you in my bed.
You said you had to go,
There were monsters in your head.

Funny little thing,
It wants to feel so much.
Just the sight of you,
It trembles with a touch.

Don't look at me that way,
Your eyes arouse a need.
Touching my face like you do,
Making it harder to breathe.
I want you,
Yes it's true.
Those eyes,
Damn are they blue.

You had it,
Her heart.
Unexpected,
From the start.

Can I just disappear?
For a little while please.
The person that they want,
I don't care to be.

Damaged goods,
Broken heart.
See her there,
Wanting to heal those parts.
You're beautiful, you know,
She'll make you see it too.
Kisses from an angel,
As she licks your wounds.

More than meets the eye,
She's the one they desire.
Seeing is believing,
She sets their hearts on fire.
But even with a good heart,
And wicked smile.
They only stay for a while.
He's out there, she said.
He'll handle every inch of her.
Forgetting those before,
Everyone, an amateur.

Someone's dream,
Maybe yours.
Just a taste,
Oh you'll want more.
Her mind so delicious,
One bites not enough.
Watch out for her,
She'll definitely call your bluff.
Mysteriously intoxicating,
You're drunk off her touch.
She'll make you feel it all,
Wanting her, is never too much.

You let them break you,
Those from your past.
Excepted their fake love,
As if it would last.

Now look at you,
A damn fool indeed.
You'll lose her you know,
If you don't see.

You tasted her,
Eyes wanting more.
Looking up at you,
Close the door.
You touched her lips,
Opening just for you.
Skin on skin,
You know what to do.
Ravenous she is,
Bite you, she might.
Give into this,
Feed her appetite.

Can't expect the sun,
If you're only giving shade.
This happiness right here,
Is mine.
Handmade.

Don't worry about her,
She will be fine.
She's as strong as they come,
Bred into her from a long line.
With wings made of patience,
She crushes your sweet pride.
Dancing to her poetry,
She can only say goodbye.
No time for hesitation,
She was meant to conquer.
Underestimate her,
Your doubt she will squander.

She waited,
For what.
The confusion,
The buts.

It's a shame,
You didn't know.
When you let her down,
She lets you go.

Unwilling to admit,
She needed him
A little bit.

You can't see it,
She hides it well.
You'd never know,
She's battling her own hell.

Caring in nature,
She wears her disguise.
Please keep in mind,
There's pain in her eyes.

A hopeless romantic,
She didn't care.
Gave into love,
Despite past despair.
Craving the rush,
The beauty of being wanted.
Needing this,
She desired to be hunted.

Walking down the street one day,
I saw a man pass my way.
He told me stories,
Which were nice.
Then out of nowhere,
He turned to ice.
His heart was broke,
From a past unknown.
Tragic is the story,
Of a heart made of stone.

Half ass attention,
That's not what I need.
With a lot on your plate,
A burden I shouldn't be.

Remember how you looked at me,
Before you let the fear set in.
I wish you knew how safe it was,
A haven from where you've been.

I'm settling you know,
For less than I deserve.
I see right through you,
Living in your hurt.
Wallow all you want,
While I pick up the pieces.
Take advantage while you can,
This game of yours is soon to cease.

Make me believe,
In something I've never seen.
I don't even know what it looks like,
Is it anything like my dreams?
How about the taste,
Could I eat it every day?
Can you show me how it feels,
Will it make me want to stay?
Maybe this is too much,
Perhaps I'm asking a lot.
I just want to know what its like,
When your heart is finally caught.

Who are you?
And where did he go.
I don't recognize,
This boy shadowing my glow.
You made the moves,
And I was along for the ride.
Little did you know?
Your rules I won't abide.
My dear, I am a woman,
It's obvious you've never had.
Should I wait for the boy to grow?
Or just leave him sad.

While you took your time,
Not knowing what to do.
Her mind began to wonder,
Why should I wait for you?

Too good for you,
She definitely was.
You're going to miss her,
And all that she does.

How would you handle a woman like me?
I'm not the delicate flower,
You thought I would be.
I play just as rough,
So watch your next move.
It'll take a damn good man,
To know how to soothe.

Impatient lover,
Take your time.
Our bodies will sync,
And you will be mine.
Kiss me slow,
Tease me right.
Soon you will feel,
This space so tight.
Take your time,
Your turn will come.
If you are patient,
You'll receive and then some.

I'm in love with the idea of love,
For I've never truly had it.
Running scared as it approaches me,
This pattern becoming a habit.
I'm in love with the idea of being in love,
A weakness I rarely share.
I think I'll remain alone for a while,
My heart I'm not willing to bare.

What will I write about today?
A woman with needs,
I crave more than I say.
My thoughts are erotic,
At times damn right dirty.
Anywhere, anyplace,
These fantasies are worthy.
A reality I wish,
But these are my dreams.
Not sharing this part of me,
None can handle it seems.
So I'll keep them to myself,
Not telling a single soul.
These secrets in the dark,
Off the tongue they long to roll.

Damn, is all I can say,
So good for me it hurts.
Can we lay under the stars?
Do we remember how this works?
Friends is all we are,
We both know I'm not ready for more.
If anyone is given that honor,
It would be you opening that door.
What I would give to know,
A touch so honest and true.
If anyone ever steals my heart,
My friend it will be you.

Friends we always say,
They laugh and shake their heads.
We are building something more,
Than just a visitor in our beds.
A classic novel,
This one we're writing.
The thing about us,
There is no hiding.
Time will tell,
Where this tale will go.
Our audience eager to see,
But you and I,
We already know.

There is something so beautiful,
About someone so deserving of love.

Wait for the hands that are strong enough to hold you
Forgetting all before.
They'll give more than you ever knew.

Completely unexpected,
This adventure shared by two.
Who would have ever thought?
Days are not the same without you.
I want to see it all,
With you by my side.
I couldn't deny this pull,
My feelings I tried to hide.
Here we are at last,
The universe feeling complete.
It was us all along,
Our paths inevitable to meet.

I waited what felt like forever for you,
Not knowing if you'd ever appear.
The universe has had plans for us,
Now all I want is to have you near.
Mountains we will climb,
Adventures we will seek.
Together hand in hand,
This passion is ours to keep.
We'll lay underneath endless stars,
Our words will come with ease.
For you and I, my dear,
We were always meant to be.

Anything at all,
You'd be there.
Feeding theses dreams,
A willing heart you share.
A soul that speaks to mine,
You're unlike any I have ever known.
Your love one day,
I hope to call my own.
Patience you have,
In me and in us.
Deserving of the stars,
A bond we're meant to trust.

There is a look about you,
I can't put my finger on it.
You are glowing you know,
I ask if you've been hit.
You look me in the eyes,
And say yes by this most beautiful piece of art.
I smile and whisper softly,
Good, this piece is my heart.
This look I can't explain,
Suddenly makes sense and now I see.
This look is one of love,
And you are looking right at me.

This will be me,
And this will be you.
Never changing who we are,
Neither one has to.
I'll look up into your eyes,
Tippy toes and all.
You'll kiss me on my forehead,
Catching each other as we fall.

He placed his hands on my face,
God, were they warm.
His presence surrounding me,
At last, my lucky charm.
As he touched the parts of me,
Using only just his voice.
I've never known such intimacy,
The outside world, just a noise.
I will get lost in you,
Never forgetting though who I am.
I will love myself always,
And I will eternally love this man.

Fairytales they called them,
You know what I mean.
Make a believer out of anyone,
A false reality that's never been seen.
Stories you've read,
Of finding the one.
An unfamiliar notion,
For your heart sat and it hung.
The tales they told are true,
This beauty had found her beast.
Behind a rough exterior,
Her thoughts he would keep.
Her mind he'd protect,
His soul she would love.
You'll know once you've seen them,
They fit each other like a glove.

Morning dew,
Brings eyes of new.
This path I am on,
Like a beautiful dawn.
An ugly lies beneath,
I feel it and its heat.
Past lives held in storage,
It will only take some courage.
To face the burdens deep,
This wicked I won't keep.
With brand new eyes,
Every morning I will rise.

I look at him,
He doesn't know.
I stare sometimes,
The sun to my soul.

Try as she might,
To fight from within.
This thing that held her,
Like the ugliest sin.
Wanting to see good,
She buried her worry.
Like ghosts they came,
Her past as it scurried.
She was what she feared,
An ugly monster full of scars.
Digging her way out,
She tried to see the stars.
Not worthy of love,
Her wounds cut to the core.
For any deserving soul,
She'd only be a bore.
Came so close,
If only she hadn't shown.
The cuts that still bleed,
A future always unknown.

Confronting the days,
With a wild and curious need.
This hunger from deep within,
She was more than ready to feed.
Be patient with yourself, she said,
As more and more started to show.
The places you wish to find,
Are buried beneath your soul.
In order to see the beauty,
You must first go through the dark.
In nature you find your peace,
For her, a good place to start.
You might not recognize parts,
Hideous in their disguise.
But you must slay your monsters,
To see beauty with brand new eyes.

He held her stare,
As she held his heart.
A love story written,
Known from the start.

Hand in hand,
As they walked through the trees.
Etched in the earth,
Their story will always be.

As the thread is pulled,
And the seams unravel.
You're lost in this place,
As the mind begins to travel.
Wicked are these stories,
You've created for yourself.
You attempt to leave the dark,
Running circles for some help.
As the words fill the page,
You start to feel empowered.
Inside a poet's mind,
Their truth never cowers.

Living in a world,
Unlike any I have found.
As they check their notifications,
Before their feet even touch the ground.
Fear of missing out,
On twitter snap and chrome.
Many times I could care less,
To even bring my phone.
I'll keep my nose in a book,
And in the dirt my hands will be.
I like my phone and all,
But the world I'd rather see.

Bars are not my thing,
The smoke if fills my lungs.
I'd rather be out back,
The words roll off my tongue.
A secret here is whispered,
Come here with the rising sun.
These words seek the truth,
This drama can't be won.
Feel the warmth of the fire,
As it brings a warm embrace.
With words that can inspire,
But actions prove this chase.

At the end of each day,
His arms are my home.
You'll find us years to come,
In a place all our own.
Riding the open roads,
The mountains in our sights.
If you'd like to come and visit,
Look for the cabin on the right.
Follow the dirt road,
That leads to the wild and the pines.
Where we rest our heads,
You won't find any street signs.

Old fashioned in nature,
My demise this will be.
It was only decades ago,
Respect was the key.
A prude I am not,
My actions may surprise you.
But I'll be damned if I succumb,
To the neediness inside you.
I hardly remember you're there,
Leaving you home all alone.
I don't even miss you that much,
You are just a silly phone.

In spite of what they think,
I'm wiser than my years.
I can't stand the color pink,
And I swallowed all my fears.
A smile I could give,
Do you need the shirt I'm wearing too?
Experienced in understanding,
Using patience as my tool.
But do not take for granted,
The kindness in my voice.
That is where you'll find,
This patience is my choice.

Write it down,
Get it out.
Look at the positive,
Remove all doubt.

Make it count,
Each thing you say.
Every thought you have,
Remember not all goes your way.
Fearless are those who continue to pursue,
Despite the shitty days.
Pick yourself up,
Remember to find time to play.
Appreciate the time to yourself,
It's few and far between.
But damn it hold onto,
The ones who love
everything about you they have seen.
Never judge a book by its cover,
The insides are usually the best.
Hold onto your gratitude,
Be different from the rest.

Find your happiness,
It's there I promise.
Deep inside the woods,
Is where I find my solace.
Master the ability,
To listen and observe.
You'll find all you need to know,
At the end of every curve.
Be patient with yourself,
You are more than you think.
Lead instead of follow,
You are the rock that never sinks.

The smile I'm wearing is mine,
One you can't take away.
No matter what I've seen,
I own each and every day.
Your ignorance I won't,
Allow to take away my harmony.
You chose your life,
And misery loves company.
Your burdens are not my own,
I won't carry them with me.
Like me or not,
I am what you see.
I care so deeply,
Pouring out empathy.
With my please and thank you's,
I need to be mindful, not all are like me.
Respect I will give when deserved,
I simply cannot fake the funk.
I've earned where I stand,
I didn't get here being a punk.

What kind of fools are we,
When we play the part.
Stand up for yourselves,
Do it from the start.
There's an art to understanding,
People and their minds.
Manipulation can grow like a weed,
Even family can take its side.
There's a power that comes from owning,
Who you are and where you'll grow.
Know what you need to flourish,
Not afraid to tell them so.
Excuses are like the wind,
Coming and going with each new day.
If you only know how to complain,
Your future will have nothing to say.

Be the bigger person,
That's what I always tell myself.
Before they raise their voice,
I remind them I am there to help.
Self-absorbed,
Story of their life.
Thinking of yourself,
Forgetting others while you strife.
Be mindful of your journey,
Not all those are the same.
The one who bares such patience,
May not always remain.

October how I love thee,
You fill me with desire.
If only Michael Myers,
Would join me by the fire.
A month of scares and haunts,
Await us every year.
Within these scary walls,
They awaken all your fears.
There's a history to be read,
And stories to be told.
Of the night the spirits wander,
Looking for lost souls.

This writer has a knack for compassion,
The ability to see what others might miss.
To give an extra smile,
To be there for the hardest hits.
Observant to every detail,
There isn't much that can't be seen.
If you watch close enough,
The bullshit could turn you mean.
Each person has a breaking point,
Will your strength overcome the masses?
Grow from every lesson,
Be nice but also be savage.